Sitting Safe in the Theatre of Electricity

Poems by Jennifer Phillips

"The mind's whispering to itself is its necessity to be itself and not to be any other..."

In honor of my teacher, poet David Ferry

Contents

Sitting Safe in the Theatre of Electricity

I love that pause when the crowd stills
here in the cinderblock amphitheatre,
the woken engine stirs,
rubber belts rumbling up the tubes
and all the small hairs, excited, rise on our necks and dance
to the Van de Graaff music.

I can feel how every electron in my cells curtsies
and starts its little backwards slide and fizzle
as the technicians of this magic
nudge their switches,
climb in the gondola of grounded steel
and we are all lifted into an inner elemental sky.

Gummy-fingered tots and minor mechanics of Lego,
mothers juggling coats and Cokes,
our neural chariots' wheels sparking on their rails
as the old gods of storm open one eye
and the torn air starts to crackle like shaken foil.

Only one infant knows to wail
at the door of mystery crashed open
between undomesticated universes
in the sneeze of light.

Home from the Pool

Punctuating the dusk

the ducks converse

        in the last circle of un-iced lake near the weir

cries like the bark of many rubber shoes on tile floor.

The footpath has thawed,

an ink-ribbon unspooled over snow,

elipses of LED lamplight receding.

No other walkers near.

The campus is on Spring break

its customary current of energy waned

like fallen water under the ice,

headed for rivers,

students confluent in hometowns distant from here,

their chat and spark,

their duffels of jeans and shirts to be washed

and folded in.

Living alone past sixty

weeks can go by and one not be touched.

The lift of air at the bare back of the neck

or a few flung drops from the breezy tamaracks

enlarges sensation

like type under a lens.

I walk often to the pool in its off-hours

to be swaddled in its surfaces,

bussed by the blue impersonal

intimacy of its skin.

Pilgrimage to Shushan, New York

Across the Walloonac River

brick and clapboard villages scant of paint

slump toward their weeds.

Cottonwoods and maple

veiled in wild grape

wall roads apart from water, woods from tarmac,

farms from their tawny seas of tall corn

where cloud-shadows

form the eddies and pools.

Seems every two-crowed dry town

or church is called Beulah or Salem,

Bethel or Shiloh

and railroads stitch together

north and south Main.

I've returned here for friends - old neighbors -

in a white frame house tucked in

to a town too small for alleys

in the bend of the Battenkill. While we were

                                        gone from each other

someone must have shifted the trunk
                              of the tattered past.
Only a few memories left like little shirts,

posed photos with parents - last post

from lovely or trying or benchmark days

before home left us just in time.

Most of those secrets got lost in rust,

oxidized away while we worked, wed,

separated, raised (or not)

children and now grandchildren.

Reality down-at-heel at last, scuffed lives

we have words for: dads who were mean

or shy or drank too much and worked too hard,

mothers who fretted, kvetched, fell sick, put up with,

scrubbed, shouted, and peeled love daily

for the tables where the six o'clock siren summoned
                              us kids up from the woods.

All the doors stick. None close entirely.

Acrimonies have lost their paint and edges.

Even the worst of memories flutter up
                              and stick to our bare legs

like locusts from the August ditches
that we can shake off and still feel thankful
kicked back on the screen porch glider,

lit by a few last Perseids passing on their ritual arc,
we three in the backyard tent
of all our years' passage, sleeping out
in the dark.

Smelling the Peaches

So much of my life

has been passed walking the dead home

snugging their sheets at dusk

putting the tiller round

until the small lights of their harbor

dwindle and distance draws them in

                    and distance draws me in

and perhaps you, too.

But now the sliced peaches tucked under their crust limpen

and even the smell is golden midsummer

from my kitchen window.

                    A stripy dragonfly

rocks on the clothesline

like the elder Wallenda on his cable over Manhattan.

                    The day itself seems poised

finding its balance

not going anywhere

as the long grass and the air's wet tongue

exchange moistures

in the bare intention of a kiss.

_____

Abba Pambo of Scete, when asked by a brother

What good thing shall I do?

answered, *Whatever you observe your soul*
to desire according to God,

do that thing.

And keep your heart safe.

Is there any safety for the heart, I wonder?

so many hearts stacked like chipped china

in a thrift shop

more every day.

And still love's flotilla bravely

sets out each sunup --

the fishers, the pleasure craft, the day-sailors,

the last-ditch rafts, the sleek and purposeful canoes.

                    Not everyone who seeks love will find it.
                    _____

The dragonfly is a hunter.

                                  She has coptered off

after some minute movement on a thread of miscanthus.

I picture her tiny eyes blazing like lasers

                                        as she zeroes in.

The desert father also said to his protégé

Be all eye like the seraphim.

So I have taken that advice to heart

on my Monet-blue Adirondack chair
                              under the summer cherry

                                      kicked back,

a whole bevvy of spirits over there, not far --

lazing somewhere under their own July trees

fingers raised to me in a neighborly way.

How painless and easy they are now in shorts and shifts and tees

enjoying like me the hills' haze

and the bees' drone over the daisies and red clover.

I know all those faces.

The prayer of the Publican is always answered.

Mercy clings to the petals of this world

new every morning and soaks our knees

and what we can't manage to find

we find we can always give away.

In Ravenna

I woke up looking for someone to tell about the light
I remembered in Ravenna.

Let me tell you:
a wash of low winter gold,

mist rising like incense
from the damp black streets.

On the rattling train ride from Rome –
oblong of receding panes,

rain, midlands plain to hilly,
smokestacks and cottages, strewn towns blurred,

much like home
like brick midlands anywhere.

Ellen, our guide,
her words precise with a creak in the back of her throat,
like a cradle by a hearth rocking,
Hebridean-American lullabies.

Pixellated color,
churches with their tympana of heaven and empire

rife with bemused saints, sheep, seraphs,
posed and snapped for a family occasion

in their grouted particulars, tinged with gold.

On the wrong side of town

           – at least by hindsight –

the Arian font reposes separate but equal in its baptistry.

The orthodoxy of those to whom the pen of history belongs

      dissolves in fog

          somewhere behind upright judicious cedars

wetting their tips in the sun's fluid

          blushing gold.

In a shop window

          a flash of goldfinches fly reflected

under a garden arch across nubile expensive shoes.

                  Time paces

rinsed and powdered to seem young for a pending reunion.

          Old bones under their altarstones

roll and stir towards each other. Radiance skews

             aslant on the foursquare

block of the golden mean as mist shakes out

          her dusty skirt, savoring

her last stolen kiss.

Positano

Travel light.

Just a spackle of words

                    to recall the stair in Positano

college kids with cameras
                  like angels ascending and
descending

between vendors of limoncello and tablecloths

      and Santa Maria Assunta, snapping themselves

or the steep street's tunnel of vines and shadows,

opening in a spangle of sea,
                  ferries nuzzling the piers

below a rabble of stacked hotels gaudy as cut fruit.

We are the luggage memory carries,

                  not the other way around.

Step back from the art-seller's collage of images

and the self-portrait starts to appear.

The next day will go on without us

                                  sky feigning innocence

clouds like wind-inflated shirts blown off their line.

                                  Mother's single stride

to tot's ten tiptoe steps

                                  our short fortnight, birth to grave

to the unending unweave and weave

a tidal grace we can't quite see the end of.

By the window, my glossary unpacks me

                                  unfold, refold the terms of passage.

Wrens pitch old sticks out of the nesting-box

                                  Some words will never inhabit this silence.

Positano lemon seeds shoot up

in the blue pot on the step

                                  Whatever we said there in the café

between the beats of the fan blades

                                  I forget.

Passion Sunday

The cryptic emperor refused to shine.

The fickle crowd stacked up like storm clouds
behind the fatal hill,

among the many things we think invisible and unreal.

It is we who rise like steam, like ghosts

to drift through the pinch and flat of what is real

the nail, the skin, the soil,

like smoke touching none of it. We pass through

with our desperate fingers, our blind eyes.

Geese trumpet over the town hall,

over the monuments and gravestones,

over the empty school,

taking their loud procession west

day after day to the gaudy lake,

not bothering with migration
from the land of the fat and warm.

A remnant of snow slumps into the lawn, soggy tissue

that sunlight decomposes under its skin of stratus.

The west wind turns around twice like an old hound
and lies down under the pines.

we are always in motion

always seeking the else and other,

the glint beyond the parliament of trees,

the flash of the lure spinning in deep water

as we follow it down.

Tide comes and goes on its own recognizance,

and now the rising winter mist eclipses

field, pond, and granite-bouldered wall

Sky chases its ball down to the shore and is gone.

Night's drop-cloth flops over us.

What was it we were reaching for?

Where did it vanish?

How did we even know to be searching?

Now stand still.

The great lung of the real breathes in and breathes out.

The great lung of the real breathes out and breathes in.

Epithalamion

Perhaps you did not see, Katie and Fernando,

                the sky's Morse message for you

on your wedding day -- the tiny puffs of cloud

                signaling delight,

the oaks opening their soft hands to you,

                the squadron of hummingbirds

saluting you on their flight-path to the rhododendrons?

The last puddles on the drive have dried.

                the just-washed grass puffs up.

The whole planet seems to swell a little

                at the sight of you, though your eyes

are only for each other.

We had all forgotten in the stale stew of daily news

                how the world is new every day,

how possibilities poke up through the soil

                and some will blossom

as you do today.

In this dessicated time that valorizes false things,

                    be only real to each other.

This morning, before the wedding, I worked an hour
                        in my garden,

            turfing out the first weeds

and hanging the deer-tape from slender stakes.

                    The tinny red of foil

is the price I pay for unchewed peonies.

                 Among the shrubbery

scarlet flashes

as though small boys with tubas

          took wrong turns from the parade.

But you two, needing no brass band, are glorious

                in your secret nuptial music

which today makes all our ears ring!

Slant Time Breathing

Thunder has us under its thumb.

Even my hair feels leaden on my head this morning.

Juniper oozes its salve over the lawn.

Trout light

                      undulating among the leaves

sends me peering into the bowl of the woods

where that which has weight without form

beds down and rises

                      moving behind the trees.

One morning, surely,

                      I will catch sight

of its dark pelt disappearing into its thickets

trailing inexorable purpose

                      like the cloy of blueberries and musk.

But now, like Elijah in the crevice

I crouch under weather's palm and wait.

———

Near abyss.

        Place where the hill's cant

slides the dish of what *is*

        toward its breaking.

I'm living on the slant

        tetchy, carrying a torch forward

squirrel-like in tiny jerks and dashes

freeze-frames in the strobe of time

        with its flashing integers

passing by in its self-importance.

Yesterday's rain smokes up like a soup-pot.

The pines recover from their two-years' drought

        quiet fireworks of new needles

thrust up against the winsome blue.

        Old LP on the turntable –
Incredible String Band's

        funky interrogatory

How long do I have to wait?

Can I get you now

                              or must I hesitate?

Wait, I think.

                    Let all this hustle pass.

Steward this window's dear acute view of the world.

Cultivate a *ten thousand mile heart*, as Li Po puts it,

                              one breath

by one breath.

Neighbors

Crow below my windowledge

jawing to siblings in the beech -

interloper at the mailbox!

Send on the alarm!

Is everyone like that these days -- scared of a stranger,

on guard, on edge?

Old speckled bird

also hollering in the weeds.

I know just what you mean.

Predators to be tempted away from nestlings.

Murder on the prowl.

Later, the whole backyard's in a ruckus.

Coyote maybe or a fox

down behind the brakeferns and goldenrod -- rustlings.

Unheard steps are the ones that mean you harm.

Bright day, only

a minor infraction of cloud.

Tomorrow, the storm.

Wind suddenly brisk from the Northeast.

Next-door flag caught out

like a lackadaisical patriot,

          now stands straight from its pole.

Weather's bound to change if you wait.

            New neighbors move in.

The way of things. Could be a blessing.

Skunk hustles close by my chair

          on her way to her hole

under the fence.

Every shifting day, we get to choose:

cower and cry danger

            or share

the delicious risk

of coinhabiting the world?

Cèilidh

Night pours out her kettle of stars,

sets out places at her table

and the dead sidle in

clutching their crinkled parchments

ready for declamation

But the reception is spotty after so much time,

fades in and out. Half an episode

dropped in the pixellation

that reveals the skull under the skin.

I only have the memories I have.

Ellen, in your Hebridean wooden boat on the whale's way

gone behind the oily swell of tide

Orpheus at the cave's mouth. It is another holy well.
                              Basalt pillars,
Lewisian pavements, thrift tufting every hollow.

A waft of your hymn lifting
                    robust through the sea's steel grille.

And such a parley of delight, Alcide,

conviction pressed with a crease

a bit of fuss, a bit of fun and gossip

then Sabbathday Lake under its kindly eiderdown of leaves

in the brisk dance of the shaking wind.

Now there's quite a crowd.

All your unrolled fragments. Scraps
                              with just a few letters,
half-stroke of the pen

the rest flaked away. Chairs scrape on the boards.

The coathooks empty. Wind comes in at the door.

Candlewicks smoke where the lovely flames

wittered and flicked out. Underneath my window

a mutter of happy voices loiters until the last comes, too.

Aubade

New day echoes *Fiat!* – up it springs
shining, gusting, swimming, creeping,
each after the way of each thing's kind
while sun's knife-blade scatters little peels of light
over the bay.

All this liveliness could come and go
as if it had never been,
mad dream of some far-off deity *pros machina,*
but for our persistent reportage,
our thumbtacking the color of April oaks
to our story-board of words,
chitter of juncos among the cedars,
hum of the hidden xylem lifting the minerals
up to the leaves.

I meant to sit with the silence for half an hour
but the mind's team is hitched and ready to run,
kit fox prances on top of the wall
a junior gymnast arched in his spotlight of joy.
Who could close their eyes
when every square inch of ground is starting out
or carrying on?

Earthworms are sucking the humus through their
                                 soft bodies under my feet

letting the air in

so the ground's chest falls and rises.

Toetips of the magnolia lift the blanket of grass.

The sleeping globe turns over

opens one eye.

                         Chionodoxa sky you could weep for

a newborn infant laid in your arms.

Take up your pen now and sing.

A Tribute of Deer

A family of deer comes drifting down the field

like a child's cutout of deer -

the stag bearing his spiked crown tall and watchful,

the perfect curve of the doe, muzzle to shoulder

nuzzling the weeds

and their fawn following, to whom the bleat of the new day

opens in wide surprise.

They pass by in early morning on their way back

from pond to forest

like a royal motorcade, while I

stand at attention on the lawn

and they barely condescend to notice.

Like any diggers-of-ditches, we

touch our caps when the mystery of beauty passes by,

three deer standing in for the whole sweep of fire.

We in the cleft of the rock, ducking like Elijah,

holding our breath so as not to see more

than God's passing backside.

They step so delicately, parsing the milkweeds,

tugging the purple vetch threads up,

tearing just a few shreds off the maple seedlings.

A desultory rain is just now

breaking into sparse snowflakes

decelerating in mid-air like slo-mo film,

then rain again.

What else can we do

but pass down the furrows with patient dignity,

pulling a few leaves from the world's tree here and there

always leaving enough for life to go on behind us,

holding our four-point rack of words up

                              like rulers of the universe,

scattering its pollen

as though all this glory was meant for us.

What You See When There Is Nothing To See

Rinsed day. May's last.

Pines with their fists of bright pins shining in slant light.

During the night an old maple fell in the wood.

                    The meaty tear of its soft core,

the rattle and thud, woke me from a convoluted dream

                        of broken and torn things.

It could not bear the weight of another Spring's canopy,

             the bulk of water drawn up to its newest tips,

the old roots losing their grip on the sodden ground.

A good way to finish --

               loaded with too much possibility to carry.

Time to let the old moorings go and make room.

                  Already a sapling is elbowing up,

preening in its new patch, widening its reach,

a toddler, center of its own universe.

———

Do you notice how the elm in the foreground

glows in its own spotlight, arranging its skirts

against the modest shadow behind,

                prima donna for a moment.

And in the matte green lawn below,

                just five blades of grass

are brandishing their light like fireflies.

We all have our moments,

                we all are brilliant in some small way

with found color or color we are found by.

              ——

The morning's bit part actors swim by.

                Some flies meander in jerks and curves,

catching gold and leaving it.

                A hornet motors down its aerial highway

long yellow legs trailing.

A jostle of midges

cloud and huddle, exchanging minute confidences

like schoolgirls on their way home.

In half an hour the sun will top the trees.

Ordinary light will open its equitable arms

and make its frank inspection of everything.

No secrets will be hid.

The day's usual errands will be done

and most of grace's visitations will become

imperceptible. But just for now

the universe is populous with its tiny lives and signals

passing by

for the witnessing of anyone who stands still.

Lunch After Gunfire

Friends came round for lunch.

Linen and late roses on the table

salmon with a coulis of sherry and dill.

They were all in

from the trenches of daily news

of letters to lawmakers, picketing the State House,

passing out hope's matches in subversive classrooms.

Up floated a time-capsule

who can say why

this particular jetsam in the drift of the past?

Proctor's Theatre, Saturday afternoon in 1965.

Sticky concrete, bristly folding seats

and Julie Andrews twirling Alp-side

above those un-nunlike nuns and gentlemanly Nazis.

My family, ice cream running between our fingers

in Central Park after the show

where willows lamented their long leaves

right into summer's scummy pond

clots of duck-down snagged at the outflow,

a whole city of crickets

raising a ruckus in the prickly grass.

How do we learn what we learn?

Later over the dishpan

stroking soap
        over the botanical plates and Sheffield stainless

I think about resistance

and buffing up the world

plate by plate, child by child,

one Saturday afternoon at a time.

We share one nature, you and I

and the man with the long gun in the mall

twins in the stroller

the mom watching the tide

of her life drain out across the tile

the young cop, dark blue stains

spreading in his armpits

the teacher staring into her cold coffee as the TV blares,

the local beat host asking the bystander

How did it feel?

We grow into who we are

by recognizing what we share.

A.J. Heschel said it best:

In this world of freedom

some are guilty but all are responsible.

A mantra for the moment

devotion a smooth stone

cradled in the palm

a cube of ice rounding on the tongue

Something to call to mind whenever

loneliness sinks its tines into us

rakes its bed of coals

and summons us to walk.

Pen Man Ship

Snow still unfallen, a sooty thumbprint overhead.

Rhododendrons rolled in their aron kodesh of snow.

Juncos spelunking under dropped limbs of pine.

A day to pen a letter out of winter's encasement

to a far-off friend, though there are faster ways

of catapulting thought.

Virtual is virtual, smoke and mirrors.

Ink is artifact, vein to vein and hand in hand,

the gap closed, of space not time,

the world in kilter and the skin in rhyme.

Brief Biography

Jennifer Phillips is an immigrant, an Episcopal Priest, a gardener, grower of Bonsai, and painter, and has been writing poetry and prose since she was seven. Born in Britain, she grew up in upstate New York and has lived in New Mexico, St. Louis, Rhode Island, and now is back in Massachusetts, where she graduated from Wellesley College and Andover Newton Theological School. She also studied at Kings College, London. Her spiritual sense and writing life have always been rooted in landscapes and their infinite changeability.

The Author may be contacted via email at revjphillips@earthlink.net

Technical Editing by Will Anderson
Bring your poetry to book form! Contact the
Technical Editor via email at wcanderson@verizon.net